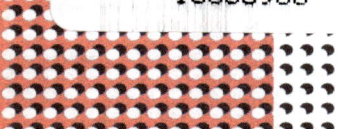

AI at Work:
A Practical Guide for Employees

"The real power of AI begins not when it thinks for us, but when it helps us think better."

**Author:
Maxwell Steinbeck**

All rights reserved.
No part of this book may be reproduced without the written permission of the author.

Publishing platform:
Amazon Kindle Direct Publishing
in 2025

Table of Content

Introduction	**4**
Chapter 1: AI Basics for Office Workers	**7**
1.1. What is artificial intelligence: basic concepts.	7
1.2. Types of AI: generative, analytical, automated.	10
1.3 Popular AI Tools: GPT-5, MidJourney, Grammarly, Notion AI, and More	14
Chapter 2: Everyday productivity with AI	**19**
2.1. Automation of routine tasks (examples: scheduling meetings, data processing).	19
2.2. Writing texts and creating reports.	22
2.3. Organization of working hours with AI assistants.	26
2.4. Data analysis and creation of visualizations.	30
Chapter 3: Teamwork with AI	**35**
3.1. Using AI for collaborative work (Google Workspace, Microsoft Copilot).	35
3.2. Communication: How AI can help with translations, letters and negotiations.	39
3.3 Tools for Project Management with AI Elements	41
Chapter 4: Ethics of using AI	**44**
4.1. Responsible use: where is the line between helping and replacing a person.	44
4.2. Issues of authorship and plagiarism when using AI.	47
4.3. Transparency: How to tell customers and colleagues about the use of AI.	50

Chapter 5: Data security when working with AI — 53
    5.1. How AI processes your data: myths and reality. — 53
    5.2. Security Best Practices: Avoiding Information Leaks. — 57
    5.3. Tools with a high level of confidentiality. — 60

Chapter 6: The Future of AI at Work — 63
    6.1. How AI is changing professions: prospects for development. — 63
    6.2. Skills worth developing to stay competitive. — 66
    6.3. How to adapt to rapid changes in technology. — 70

    Appendices — 73

Introduction

What is artificial intelligence? At first glance, it may still seem like something complex and highly technical, yet AI has quietly become the invisible engine of modern life. Every time we unlock a smartphone with facial recognition, search for information online, or receive a playlist on Spotify that fits our mood, we are interacting with intelligent systems that learn, predict, and adapt. Artificial intelligence is no longer a futuristic concept — it is an active participant in how we work, communicate, and create value.

In the workplace, AI's potential has moved from theoretical to practical. Tasks that once consumed hours — writing reports, managing calendars, analyzing data, or summarizing meetings — can now be handled by AI assistants integrated directly into office tools such as Microsoft Copilot, Google Workspace AI, Notion AI, and Zoom AI Companion. These systems automate repetitive work, freeing employees to focus on what humans do best: creativity, strategy, empathy, and problem-solving. The shift is not only operational but also cultural — AI is redefining how we collaborate, learn, and make decisions.

For today's workforce, understanding AI is as important as computer literacy was at the dawn of the internet. The pace of technological change is extraordinary. Large language models like GPT-5, Claude 3.5, Gemini 2, and open-source systems like LLaMA 3 don't just answer questions—they act as intelligent partners that can reason, plan, and adapt to context. To thrive in this environment, employees don't need to become data scientists or programmers. What's important is knowing how these systems think, how to use them responsibly, and how to integrate them into everyday workflows.

Across every profession, AI is expanding human capability. Marketers can analyze consumer behavior in real time and generate personalized campaigns. Project managers use AI agents to forecast risks, track progress, and optimize resources. Lawyers review hundreds of pages of contracts in minutes with AI-driven document analysis. Designers and writers collaborate with creative AI tools that assist in concept generation, visual prototyping, and editing. Even in agriculture and small business, AI now helps monitor soil quality, manage supply chains, and forecast market trends.

These transformations inevitably raise concerns — especially about automation and job security. Yet history shows that each technological revolution reshapes work rather than eliminates it. Just as the printing press, the steam engine, and the computer once redefined labor, AI is ushering in a new era of partnership between humans and machines. Routine tasks are disappearing, but in their place arise more analytical, creative, and meaningful roles. Accountants become strategic advisors. Customer-service representatives evolve into relationship managers. New professions — such as AI coordinator, prompt strategist, and ethical AI consultant — are emerging to guide this collaboration.

Artificial intelligence also reimagines teamwork. It enables seamless communication across departments, languages, and time zones. With shared AI dashboards and collaborative agents, teams can co-create documents, analyze complex data, or brainstorm ideas simultaneously, regardless of location. This not only accelerates decision-making but also fosters inclusion, as AI tools can instantly translate, summarize, or adjust information to different learning styles and languages.

A defining feature of AI is its capacity to learn. Unlike traditional software that executes fixed commands, AI systems continuously improve through feedback, learning from each interaction to deliver smarter and more relevant outcomes. This self-improving nature means that, over time, AI becomes an increasingly valuable collaborator — one that adapts to personal working styles and organizational goals.

With this power comes responsibility. Ethical use of AI is no longer optional—it is a professional standard. Global regulations set clear expectations for transparency, data privacy, and accountability. Workers and companies must learn to safely deploy AI, ensuring that automation serves human needs, not undermines them. Understanding where to draw the line—between assistance and overdependence, between innovation and intrusion—is now part of digital literacy.

AI is also transforming how we learn. Instead of one-size-fits-all training, AI-driven education platforms identify each learner's strengths and weaknesses and tailor courses accordingly. Whether you want to master leadership, communication, or data analysis, AI-powered systems guide you through personalized learning paths that adapt in real time, making professional development more efficient and engaging.

Ultimately, understanding AI is no longer just a technical advantage — it is a foundation for modern career resilience. Artificial intelligence is not replacing people; it is empowering them to think, create, and contribute at a higher level. Mastering it is not about coding but about collaboration — learning to work *with* intelligence, not *against* it. Those who embrace this change will not only keep pace with the future of work — they will help shape it.

Chapter 1:
AI Basics for Office Workers

1.1. What is artificial intelligence: basic concepts.

Artificial intelligence, or AI, is a technology that has become an integral part of modern life, shaping how we work, communicate, and create value. At its core, AI refers to systems designed to perform tasks that traditionally require human intelligence — from speech recognition and data analysis to decision-making and even creative problem-solving. For office workers and professionals, understanding AI's basic concepts is essential, as it enables them to harness these tools effectively to improve productivity and innovation.

AI can be thought of as a versatile, adaptive tool that learns to tackle different tasks efficiently. It operates through algorithms — sets of instructions that guide how information is processed. For example, AI systems can analyze vast datasets to identify patterns, predict outcomes, and suggest actionable insights. In office environments, this means automating labor-intensive processes like data aggregation, report generation, or document classification, allowing employees to focus on higher-level strategy and creative work.

A key component of artificial intelligence is machine learning (ML). Machine learning allows systems to learn from historical data and improve over time. In practice, email platforms use ML to automatically detect spam or categorize messages. In offices, ML can streamline workflows such as routing customer support tickets, sorting documents, and pre-analytics. Advanced AI tools now include reinforcement learning and continuous learning, which allows agents to dynamically adapt to changing tasks without explicit reprogramming.

Another fundamental aspect is natural language processing (NLP), which allows AI to understand, interpret, and generate human language. Modern AI assistants, chatbots, and writing tools can summarize meetings, draft emails, translate documents, or even analyze team sentiment from internal communications. NLP now underpins many productivity tools like Microsoft Copilot, Notion AI, and Zoom AI Companion, enabling employees to interact naturally with AI systems across multiple platforms.

Computer vision extends AI's capabilities to visual data. By recognizing and analyzing images, videos, or even complex visual patterns, AI can support marketing campaigns, design workflows, and document management. For example, office teams can automatically tag images, extract text from scanned documents, or analyze visual feedback from clients. In agriculture and small business, computer vision helps monitor inventory, track production, or assess product quality.

At the foundation of these capabilities are neural networks — mathematical models inspired by the human brain. Neural networks consist of interconnected nodes that process complex information, enabling breakthroughs in speech recognition, image analysis, and generative AI tasks like content creation. In office applications, neural networks support predictive analytics, customer behavior modeling, and even creative ideation.

Artificial intelligence also encompasses expert systems, which use knowledge bases and logical rules to aid decision-making. Lawyers, financial analysts, and project managers can benefit from expert systems that evaluate legal documents, optimize resources, or suggest strategic solutions. Modern AI agents now integrate multiple expert systems and autonomously coordinate tasks across different platforms, further increasing efficiency.

It is crucial to understand that AI complements rather than replaces humans. By automating routine and repetitive tasks, employees can dedicate their time to creative, strategic, and high-impact work. For example, AI can generate initial reports, draft presentations, or process data, while humans focus on interpretation, innovation, and relationship-building.

The ethical and responsible use of AI is equally important. Office professionals must consider data privacy, transparency, and bias reduction when deploying AI tools. Regulations set clear rules for fairness, accountability, and worker safety. Understanding these principles ensures that AI systems are used appropriately, protecting both organizations and individuals while maximizing productivity.

1.2. Types of AI: generative, analytical, automated.

Artificial intelligence can take different forms, each designed for specific tasks and professional needs. Understanding these types and knowing how to start using them allows employees, small business owners, and professionals to maximize productivity and creativity.

Generative AI

What it does:
  Generative AI creates new content based on existing data — including text, images, audio, video, and even code.

Practical applications:
- Marketing: Generate personalized ad copy, social media posts, or email campaigns.

- Design: Quickly prototype graphics, presentations, or UX/UI concepts.
- Content creation: Draft articles, reports, scripts, or routine correspondence.
- Software development: Auto-generate code snippets or documentation.

How to start using it:

1. **Choose one platform:** Start with a familiar tool such as GPT-5 for text, Canva Magic Studio for visuals, or Notion AI for document workflows.
2. **Test on small projects:** Automate simple content tasks (e.g., draft meeting summaries, social media captions).
3. **Integrate gradually:** Connect the AI tool to your existing productivity ecosystem (email, project management, Slack, Notion).
4. **Set review processes:** Always validate output to maintain quality and accuracy.

Best practices:

- Begin with repetitive or time-consuming tasks to gain confidence.
- Use prompts strategically to guide AI toward desired outputs.
- Document workflows for team consistency and scalability.

Analytical AI

What it does:
Analytical AI collects, processes, and interprets large volumes of data, finding patterns, forecasting trends, and recommending actions.

Practical applications:

- Finance: Automate budgeting, forecasting, and risk assessment.
- HR: Optimize scheduling, performance analysis, and recruitment.
- Sales & Marketing: Identify high-potential leads, forecast demand, optimize campaigns.
- Operations: Improve logistics, inventory management, and resource allocation.

How to start using it:

1. **Identify a key process:** Pick an area where data analysis can bring immediate benefits (e.g., sales performance or staff scheduling).
2. **Choose the right tools:** Microsoft Copilot Insights, Tableau AI, or specialized industry platforms for analytics.
3. **Prepare data:** Ensure data is clean, organized, and privacy-compliant.
4. **Interpret results:** Teach your team how to read AI-generated insights and apply them to decisions.

Best practices:

- Start with one high-impact dataset and expand gradually.
- Combine with automated AI to act on insights (e.g., trigger automated emails or reports).
- Regularly review AI predictions against real outcomes to validate accuracy.

Automated AI

What it does:
Automated AI handles standardized, repetitive tasks that would normally require human effort. It executes these reliably and efficiently, freeing humans for more creative and strategic work.

Practical applications:
- Customer support: Chatbots provide instant responses to FAQs.
- Accounting: Automated invoice processing, payroll calculations, and reporting.
- Inventory: Smart systems reorder stock when levels drop below thresholds.
- Scheduling: Calendar management and task reminders.

How to start using it:
1. **Identify repetitive tasks:** Map out processes that are time-consuming yet rule-based.
2. **Select automation tools:** Slack GPT, Power Automate, Zapier AI, or integrated AI agents in office platforms.
3. **Test on small processes:** Start with a single workflow (e.g., automated meeting reminders or simple report generation).
4. **Scale gradually:** Once confident, expand automation across departments or projects.

Best practices:
- Always monitor AI outputs for errors or exceptions.
- Combine automated AI with analytical and generative AI for optimal efficiency.

- Train employees on how to supervise and collaborate with AI systems.

Combining AI Types for Maximum Impact

Generative, analytical, and automated AI are most powerful when used together:

- Analytical AI identifies areas for improvement and potential automation.
- Automated AI handles repetitive tasks based on analytical insights.
- Generative AI creates content, templates, or scripts to support workflows.

Example workflow for office or small business:

1. Analytical AI forecasts upcoming tasks or customer needs.
2. Automated AI executes routine tasks (emails, orders, or reporting).
3. Generative AI produces supporting documents, presentations, or creative content.

This combined approach allows employees to focus on strategic, creative, and human-centered work, improving efficiency, accuracy, and innovation.

1.3 Popular AI Tools: GPT-5, MidJourney, Grammarly, Notion AI, and More

In today's workplace, AI tools have become indispensable for enhancing productivity, creativity, and efficiency. Popular platforms like GPT-5, MidJourney, Grammarly, and Notion AI, along with new tools, offer employees practical ways to streamline work and innovate. Understanding how to apply these tools effectively can transform daily workflows.

GPT-5 (Text and Content Generation)

GPT-5, developed by OpenAI, is the latest generation of AI text models. It helps users generate content, answer questions, brainstorm ideas, and draft professional communications.

Practical applications:

- Writing emails, reports, proposals, and marketing copy.
- Summarizing documents or extracting key insights.
- Brainstorming new ideas for campaigns, presentations, or projects.

Getting started:

1. Identify routine writing tasks that consume significant time.
2. Test GPT-5 with prompts tailored to your department or workflow.
3. Review AI outputs for quality and context before use.

Best practices:

- Use GPT-5 to augment, not replace, human judgment.
- Combine with analytical AI for data-driven content creation.

- Establish internal standards for prompt formatting to maintain consistency.

MidJourney (Visual Content Creation)

MidJourney specializes in AI-powered visual content, making it ideal for design, marketing, and presentation teams. It can generate images, infographics, and professional graphics from textual prompts.

Practical applications:

- Creating marketing visuals and social media content.
- Designing presentations and promotional materials.
- Producing concept art or mood boards for creative projects.

Getting started:

1. Experiment with simple prompts to generate visuals.
2. Use templates and customization features to align outputs with branding.
3. Integrate outputs with platforms like Canva or Adobe tools for final edits.

Best practices:

- Always validate generated visuals for brand consistency and inclusivity.
- Encourage collaboration by sharing AI-generated assets with team members.
- Track effective prompts to build an internal library for future projects.

Grammarly (Writing Assistance)

Grammarly remains a core tool for professional communication, helping ensure clarity, tone, and correctness. The 2025 version now integrates AI-assisted suggestions for style, conciseness, and audience-specific tone adjustments.

Practical applications:

- Improving emails, proposals, and internal reports.
- Tailoring communication for different audiences (formal, casual, persuasive).
- Maintaining consistency across team documents.

Getting started:

1. Integrate Grammarly with email, document editors, and communication platforms.
2. Set organizational tone and style preferences for team-wide consistency.
3. Use suggestions to enhance readability, but always review for context.

Best practices:

- Combine Grammarly with GPT-5 to draft and refine content efficiently.
- Use Grammarly insights for team writing skill development.

Notion AI (Productivity and Workflow Automation)

Notion AI extends the popular Notion productivity platform with AI-powered assistance for content generation, workflow management, and project organization.

Practical applications:
- Summarizing long documents or meeting notes.
- Drafting agendas, task lists, and project plans.
- Supporting collaborative content creation in real-time.

Getting started:
1. Identify recurring documentation or project management tasks.
2. Use Notion AI to automate summaries, reminders, and drafts.
3. Encourage team members to interact with AI suggestions for collaboration.

Best practices:
- Use AI to reduce repetitive work while retaining human oversight.
- Establish internal templates and guidelines for AI-assisted projects.

Other Tools to Consider

- **Microsoft Copilot:** Embedded AI assistant across Office apps for automated document drafting, data analysis, and workflow suggestions.
- **Slack GPT:** Context-aware AI for team communication, summarizing threads, and generating task reminders.
- **Canva Magic Studio:** AI-powered creative suite for marketing and design teams, combining generative visuals with branding templates.
- **Zoom AI Companion:** Real-time meeting summaries, action item extraction, and transcription.

Practical integration tips:
1. Begin with one tool per workflow to avoid overwhelm.
2. Pilot with a small team, then expand based on feedback.
3. Combine generative, analytical, and automated AI where possible to maximize efficiency.

Mastering these tools not only saves time but also unlocks new possibilities for creativity, decision-making, and strategic thinking. Employees who integrate AI thoughtfully gain a competitive advantage while maintaining human oversight and ethical responsibility.

Chapter 2:
Everyday productivity with AI

2.1. Automation of routine tasks (examples: scheduling meetings, data processing).

In today's fast-paced workplace, AI-driven automation has become an essential tool for increasing efficiency, reducing stress, and freeing employees to focus on creative and strategic work. Routine tasks—such as scheduling meetings, processing data, and managing workflows—can now be automated reliably using modern AI tools and intelligent integrations.

Meeting Scheduling and Calendar Management

Scheduling meetings, while seemingly simple, is often time-consuming. Coordinating participants across time zones, finding free slots, and sending reminders can take hours each week. AI now streamlines this process:

Tools & Examples:

- **Microsoft Copilot** and **Google Calendar AI** can automatically suggest optimal meeting times, generate video call links, and adjust for participants' time zones.

- **Calendly AI** and **Doodle AI** can handle invitations, send reminders, and even propose alternative times if conflicts arise.

- **Zoom AI Companion** can suggest agendas and follow-up actions based on prior meeting notes.

Getting started:
1. Connect your calendar to AI-assisted scheduling tools.
2. Let the system recommend available slots automatically.
3. Review and confirm suggestions, adding personal preferences if needed.

Benefits:
- Saves hours of coordination per week.
- Reduces missed or late meetings.
- Ensures seamless virtual collaboration for remote or hybrid teams.

Data Processing and Analysis

AI automation excels in handling large volumes of data, which can otherwise overwhelm employees. Financial analysis, marketing reports, customer insights, and operational metrics can all be processed faster and more accurately.

Tools & Examples:
- **GPT-5 and Claude 3.5** can summarize complex documents, extract insights, and generate actionable reports.
- **Microsoft Copilot Excel** can automatically clean data, identify trends, and forecast results.
- **AI-powered analytics platforms** (Tableau AI, Notion AI with workflow automation) help teams visualize and interpret data quickly.

Practical applications:
- Marketing teams can use AI to analyze customer behavior, predict engagement, and optimize campaigns.

- Finance teams can forecast revenue, automate bookkeeping, and identify anomalies.
- Operations teams can streamline production, inventory, and quality control using computer vision and predictive AI.

Getting started:

1. Identify high-volume repetitive tasks in your workflow.
2. Pilot AI tools on a small dataset.
3. Train employees on interpreting AI-generated insights responsibly.

Workflow and Operational Automation

Beyond meetings and data, AI now automates broader operational workflows:

- **Customer service:** AI chatbots handle inquiries 24/7, freeing human agents for complex cases.
- **Inventory management:** AI predicts stock shortages and automatically triggers reorders.
- **HR and compliance:** AI assists with onboarding, timesheet verification, and document review.

Getting started:

1. Map repetitive processes suitable for automation.
2. Introduce AI gradually, combining automated actions with human supervision.
3. Monitor outcomes to ensure quality, accuracy, and compliance.

Benefits:

- Increases productivity and reduces errors.

- Allows employees to focus on strategic, creative, and high-value tasks.
- Enhances operational consistency and compliance with ethical standards.

Ethical Considerations and Data Privacy

Automation comes with responsibilities. AI systems process sensitive corporate and personal data, so ethical and legal compliance is critical:

- Ensure adherence to the EU AI Act, GDPR, and local privacy laws.
- Avoid over-reliance on AI decisions without human oversight.
- Regularly audit AI outputs for bias, fairness, and accuracy.

Tip: Educate employees on proper usage, data privacy, and ethical practices to maintain trust and accountability.

2.2. Writing texts and creating reports.

Writing documents, reports, and content remains a central part of daily work for many employees, whether in marketing, finance, education, or operations. While some writing is routine, other tasks demand creativity and high precision. Regardless, all can consume substantial time—especially when processing large volumes of data or ensuring accuracy in structured documents.

Artificial intelligence (AI) now dramatically improves this process, helping employees create high-quality texts and reports more efficiently. From drafting and editing to analyzing data and generating visualizations, AI opens new opportunities for productivity while allowing workers to focus on strategic and creative tasks.

AI for Text Generation

Modern generative AI systems, such as GPT-5, Claude 3.5, and LLaMA 3, can generate text tailored to specific topics, styles, or company guidelines.

Practical Applications:

- Writing quarterly financial reports by summarizing raw data and highlighting trends.
- Generating marketing copy, blog posts, or internal newsletters.
- Drafting proposals, emails, or training materials with consistent tone and structure.

Getting Started:

1. Define the purpose and audience for your text.
2. Provide clear prompts with context (e.g., data, style preferences).
3. Review and refine AI-generated drafts to ensure accuracy and alignment with goals.

Benefits:

- Reduces time spent drafting texts.
- Maintains logical structure and high readability.
- Enables rapid iteration and content variation.

AI for Editing and Proofreading

AI tools now offer advanced grammar, spelling, stylistic, and clarity suggestions. Systems such as Grammarly Premium, Microsoft Editor with Copilot integration, and Writer AI can detect subtle errors, suggest word choice improvements, and adapt recommendations to different communication contexts.

Practical Applications:

- Ensuring professional tone in emails, proposals, and reports.
- Standardizing style across multiple authors in team projects.
- Improving readability and accessibility of marketing and training materials.

Getting Started:

1. Integrate AI editing tools with your writing platform.
2. Review AI suggestions critically—accept changes that enhance clarity and style.
3. Combine AI feedback with human judgment for creative and nuanced content.

Benefits:

- Enhances accuracy and professionalism.
- Maintains stylistic consistency across documents.
- Reduces time spent on manual proofreading.

AI for Data-Driven Reports

Employees often need to transform large datasets into insightful reports. AI now handles not just number crunching but also textual summarization and visualization.

Tools & Applications:

- **GPT-5 and Claude 3.5** for summarizing datasets and generating narrative reports.
- **Microsoft Copilot Excel** for automated data cleaning, trend analysis, and forecasting.

- **Notion AI and Tableau AI** for generating charts, graphs, and dashboards directly from datasets.

Practical Applications:

- Finance: Automating revenue, expense, and investment analysis with predictive insights.
- Marketing: Transforming user behavior data into recommendations for campaign optimization.
- Operations: Creating visual reports on production, inventory, or quality metrics.

Getting Started:

1. Identify repetitive reporting tasks suitable for automation.
2. Connect your data sources to AI tools and generate preliminary drafts.
3. Validate AI-generated insights before finalizing reports to ensure accuracy.

Benefits:

- Speeds up report creation from hours to minutes.
- Reduces human errors in data interpretation.
- Supports informed, data-driven decision-making.

Team Collaboration and Multilingual Writing

AI assists in maintaining consistency when multiple employees work on the same project. In multinational teams, AI-powered translation tools such as DeepL, GPT-5 multilingual mode, and Google Translate Pro allow rapid, accurate translation of reports and marketing materials.

Practical Applications:
- Harmonizing style and structure in collaborative documents.
- Translating reports, presentations, and customer communications for global audiences.
- Generating multilingual content without outsourcing to translators.

Getting Started:
1. Establish a team style guide and share it with AI tools.
2. Use AI to draft, translate, and harmonize content collaboratively.
3. Encourage human review to ensure context and nuance are preserved.

Benefits:
- Ensures professional consistency across teams.
- Supports international business operations.
- Reduces costs and time for multilingual content creation.

2.3. Organization of working hours with AI assistants.

Artificial intelligence has quietly become a new kind of colleague — one that never gets tired, never loses focus, and works on your schedule. The challenge today is not just to *use* AI, but to organize your workday around it so that human creativity and digital precision complement each other.

Rethinking the Workday

Most employees still organize their day in the same way they did before AI — long to-do lists, time blocks, endless context switching. But AI assistants thrive on structure and clarity. When your workday is aligned with how AI processes information, productivity can double without working harder.

Start by dividing your daily tasks into two categories:

- **Cognitive and creative tasks** – writing, strategy, analysis, problem-solving.
- **Procedural and repetitive tasks** – scheduling, reporting, formatting, information search.

AI can take full responsibility for the second category and assist with the first. For example, an employee can dictate a project outline to ChatGPT or Notion AI in the morning, then let the assistant prepare drafts, find sources, or generate summaries while focusing on meetings or fieldwork.

The "AI-Assisted Flow" Technique

One effective model is to treat your AI assistant as a co-pilot in a four-phase workflow:

1. **Plan Together** — Begin each day with a short AI planning session. Ask your assistant to generate a daily agenda based on your goals, deadlines, and energy peaks. Tools: ChatGPT, Microsoft 365 Copilot, Motion, or Reclaim.ai.

2. **Delegate Routine** — Let AI handle repetitive or low-value work: draft emails, summarize long documents, or create data visualizations.

3. **Co-Create** — Use generative AI for brainstorming, design, or strategy sessions. It works best when you provide examples and constraints — that's how AI produces relevant, refined outcomes.

4. **Review and Reflect** — End the day by reviewing progress with your assistant: what tasks were completed, what

patterns appeared, what can be automated tomorrow. This creates a self-improving cycle.

When practiced regularly, this rhythm builds what psychologists call "cognitive offloading" — transferring non-essential tasks to machines so that your brain stays focused on decisions, relationships, and creativity.

Practical Tools to Structure Your Day

AI-assisted productivity no longer requires complex setups. Here are practical tools many professionals use:

- **AI Schedulers** (Motion, Clockwise, Reclaim.ai) — automatically rearrange meetings and breaks to maintain focus blocks.
- **Intelligent Notebooks** (Notion AI, Mem.ai) — generate summaries, meeting notes, or idea structures instantly.
- **Automation Hubs** (Zapier, Make, Power Automate) — link different applications so that repetitive actions happen automatically.
- **Focus Companions** (Cortext, ChatGPT, or custom voice assistants) — help you prioritize, remind, and track energy levels throughout the day.

The secret is not in the number of tools, but in how intentionally they are combined. For example, scheduling software that syncs with your AI note-taker can automatically insert time to process ideas or prepare reports — before deadlines arrive.

Energy Management Meets AI

Time management is no longer enough; in the age of AI, energy management becomes the new currency of productivity.
AI tools can track your performance rhythms — when you write best, when your attention drops — and suggest when to switch

tasks or rest.

Applications like Rise or Timeular visualize your energy curve and recommend optimal timing for deep work, meetings, or creative sessions.

When used correctly, AI doesn't just make you faster — it helps you work in sync with your natural cycles, preventing burnout and decision fatigue.

From Time Control to Time Design

Before AI, productivity meant discipline and control. Now it's about design — crafting a workday that blends human focus with digital automation.

Instead of "fighting the clock," employees can design intelligent days where AI anticipates needs, prevents overload, and keeps creativity flowing.

In practice, this might look like:

- 9:00 — AI summarizes your unread messages and drafts replies.
- 10:00 — Deep focus session supported by an AI blocker that silences non-urgent notifications.
- 13:00 — AI-assisted lunch check-in that tracks calories or suggests mindful breaks.
- 16:00 — Quick AI debrief summarizing achievements and generating tomorrow's plan.

When such patterns are repeated, the line between "working" and "being managed by technology" dissolves. What remains is a seamless flow — human intuition guided by artificial intelligence.

2.4. Data analysis and creation of visualizations.

In today's data-driven workplace, information has become the most valuable form of capital — yet it only has value when it can be clearly understood and acted upon.

Artificial intelligence now makes this process faster, more intuitive, and more accessible than ever. What once required a team of analysts can now be done by a single employee working with intelligent assistants.

From Data to Decisions

Every organization — from local farms to global enterprises — produces enormous volumes of information: sales records, financial reports, employee performance data, or customer feedback. But data in raw form is like unrefined ore. Its true worth appears only after it has been cleaned, structured, and interpreted.

AI systems are now deeply integrated into this analytical chain.
Modern tools powered by GPT-5, Claude 3.5, Gemini 2, or Microsoft Copilot can automatically process large datasets, identify anomalies, fill in missing values, and detect outliers long before they distort results.

These assistants not only accelerate the "data cleaning" stage but also learn from historical corrections, improving accuracy with every project.

For example, Copilot for Excel can now flag inconsistent financial records or duplicate transactions automatically, while Notion AI or Airtable Smart Fields can clean and label unstructured data coming from surveys or customer forms. Such automation reduces human error and saves hours of manual work.

Selecting the Right Analytical Model

Once the data is prepared, the next task is to extract meaning.
AI tools can now autonomously recommend analytical models — classification, regression, clustering, or even deep learning — depending on your goal. You no longer need to be a statistician to uncover trends.

- **Predictive analysis** helps forecast future sales, demand, or prices.
- **Descriptive analysis** reveals what has happened and why.
- **Diagnostic analysis** pinpoints the cause of anomalies or drops in performance.

Autonomous AI agents, such as ChatGPT Advanced Data Analysis or Gemini 2 Data Explorer, can run multi-step analyses in the background, generate hypotheses, and even create draft reports in natural language.

These systems combine machine learning with reasoning — turning numbers into explanations.

Visualization: Making Data Speak

Data has little impact until it is seen.
Visualization transforms abstract patterns into visual narratives that everyone — from managers to clients — can understand. In 2025, AI has revolutionized this process.

Platforms like Power BI with Copilot, Tableau Pulse, and Google Looker Studio can now generate complete dashboards automatically. The AI analyzes your dataset, determines the most informative metrics, and recommends the right visualization:
bar charts for comparisons, line graphs for trends, heat maps for geographic distribution, or bubble charts for correlations.

Meanwhile, creative tools such as Canva Magic Studio and ChatGPT Canvas Charts allow users with no design background to create presentation-ready visuals that match brand aesthetics automatically.

Interactive and Adaptive Dashboards

One of the most powerful advances is interactivity.
Modern dashboards are not static reports but living systems.
Managers can ask natural-language questions — "Show me sales growth in Q3 across rural regions" — and AI instantly filters, visualizes, and narrates the result.

Users can adjust parameters, drill down into regions or timeframes, and see how patterns evolve in real time.

This shift from static charts to dynamic exploration is transforming decision-making.

Instead of passively receiving data, employees can now "converse" with it — refining questions and discovering insights collaboratively with their AI assistants.

Predictive and Prescriptive Analytics

Beyond understanding the past, AI helps anticipate the future.
Machine learning models trained on historical data can forecast demand, identify risks, and suggest the best actions.
For instance:

- In agriculture, AI predicts crop yields or pest outbreaks based on weather and soil data.
- In retail, it anticipates customer demand and optimizes inventory levels.
- In finance, it detects fraud patterns or forecasts market fluctuations.

The latest generation of tools — like Claude 3.5 Predictive Models or GPT-5 Code Interpreter — can also simulate "what-if" scenarios, helping teams evaluate strategies before implementing them. This turns analytics from a reactive process into a proactive management system.

Discovering Hidden Patterns

Perhaps the most transformative feature of AI analysis is pattern discovery.

AI models can detect subtle correlations invisible to traditional statistical methods — for example, links between employee engagement and customer retention, or between regional weather patterns and sales cycles.

These insights allow organizations to make data-informed decisions rooted not in intuition, but in empirical understanding.

Visualization plays a crucial role here. Heat maps, correlation matrices, and temporal animations translate complex relationships into intuitive visual form. A well-designed chart can reveal in seconds what might take hours to explain in a spreadsheet.

Automation and Integration

Most analytical workflows have become multi-tool ecosystems.
AI orchestrators like Zapier AI, Make.com Agents, and Microsoft Power Automate with Copilot can gather data from emails, CRMs, sensors, and spreadsheets — then feed it into analysis models and generate reports automatically.
These automated pipelines allow professionals to focus not on data handling, but on insights and strategy.

For small businesses or freelancers, lightweight solutions such as ChatGPT Workspace Analytics or Notion AI Dashboards make it possible to monitor financial health, marketing performance, or project progress in a single conversational interface.

Practical Takeaways

- **Start small but automate early.** Even basic automation in data cleaning saves hours weekly.
- **Visualize for understanding, not decoration.** Every chart should answer a question, not just display information.
- **Collaborate with your AI.** Treat it as a thinking partner that helps refine questions and discover unexpected insights.
- **Keep the human in the loop.** AI amplifies intelligence, but interpretation and context remain human strengths.

Thanks to these advancements, AI-powered analytics has become not just a technical process but a universal workplace language.

Employees, entrepreneurs, and researchers can now see patterns, forecast outcomes, and communicate ideas more clearly than ever — turning data into understanding, and understanding into intelligent action.

Chapter 3:

Teamwork with AI

3.1. Using AI for collaborative work (Google Workspace, Microsoft Copilot).

The integration of artificial intelligence into collaborative work has reshaped how modern teams operate. We live in a time when AI will no longer be just a useful add-on, but will become a silent team member, supporting planning, communication, and creativity at every stage of a project. Platforms like Google Workspace with Duet AI, Microsoft 365 with Copilot, and newer tools like Notion AI, Slack GPT, and Zoom AI Companion have transformed everyday teamwork into a more dynamic, efficient, and less stressful process.

From Tools to Intelligent Ecosystems

Modern collaboration platforms are no longer isolated applications — they are connected ecosystems where text, data, and communication flow seamlessly.

- **Google Workspace with Duet AI** assists in document creation, automatically summarizes meeting notes, and generates action items from discussions. In Google Docs, real-time writing suggestions now adapt to your team's tone and style, while Google Meet provides live summaries and task tracking that sync with Google Tasks.

- **Microsoft Copilot for 365**, deeply integrated into Word, Excel, PowerPoint, and Outlook, functions as an intelligent colleague. It drafts reports, extracts insights from spreadsheets, creates slide decks, and manages inboxes with contextual understanding. In Excel, for instance, Copilot now detects data trends automatically, builds predictive dashboards, and suggests next steps based on past team decisions.

These systems have evolved from being assistants to becoming collaboration orchestrators — connecting inputs from multiple people and tools into one cohesive workflow.

Practical Applications in Everyday Teamwork

In real-world practice, teams now use AI to coordinate, communicate, and create at scale:

- **Brainstorming and Ideation:** Teams generate structured ideas using AI-powered whiteboards (Miro AI, Notion AI Brainstorm), which cluster suggestions by themes and feasibility.
- **Document Collaboration:** Shared documents become living workspaces — AI highlights inconsistencies, tracks progress, and even rewrites sections for clarity or brand tone.
- **Project Management:** AI agents in tools like Asana, ClickUp, and Trello analyze workloads, detect bottlenecks, and rebalance tasks automatically.
- **Meetings and Communication:** Zoom AI Companion and Slack GPT summarize discussions, propose follow-up tasks, and link them directly to project boards — ensuring that every conversation leads to measurable outcomes.

How to Start Integrating AI Collaboration Tools

Implementing AI teamwork doesn't require an overhaul — it's best approached step by step:

1. **Identify repetitive tasks** — such as reporting, note-taking, or email sorting — and let AI handle them first.
2. **Integrate one ecosystem** (Google or Microsoft) instead of mixing too many apps at once. This minimizes confusion and ensures compatibility.
3. **Train the team** — hold short internal sessions to show real examples of AI in use. Productivity grows when employees see direct benefits, not just abstract promises.
4. **Set guidelines for collaboration** — define when to rely on AI (e.g., drafting reports) and when human review is essential (e.g., final decisions, client communication).
5. **Monitor and adapt** — measure which tools save time and which create friction, and adjust your workflows accordingly.

By viewing AI as a collaborative framework rather than a single tool, teams learn to design workflows that amplify human insight while reducing administrative overhead.

Cross-Department Collaboration

AI has become the bridge between departments that used to work in silos.

Marketing teams use Gemini for Workspace or ChatGPT for Enterprise to analyze campaign data; sales teams instantly access those insights in Excel dashboards; customer service integrates chat summaries into CRM systems. This kind of real-time data sharing creates transparency and aligns goals across the organization — something that manual reporting could never achieve efficiently.

Human Impact: Reducing Stress, Increasing Flow

AI collaboration tools help reduce digital overload. By offloading repetitive coordination tasks, employees regain time for deep work — thinking, problem-solving, and innovation. Teams report lower stress levels, clearer communication, and fewer "lost" tasks. Instead of multitasking between chats, spreadsheets, and notes, workers now interact through a unified, intelligent workspace that keeps everything connected.

Key Takeaways

- **AI is now a co-worker, not just software.** It supports, suggests, and connects — improving both speed and quality of teamwork.
- **Start small, scale smart.** Focus on one area (like meeting notes or reporting) and expand as your team's comfort grows.
- **Balance automation with human judgment.** Use AI to handle structure and data, while people provide context, empathy, and creativity.
- **Measure impact.** Successful AI adoption is visible when teams spend less time managing tasks and more time creating value.

Today, AI-powered collaboration is not about replacing human effort, but about redistributing it to what really matters: understanding, innovation, and meaningful human connection.

3.2. Communication: How AI can help with translations, letters and negotiations.

Artificial intelligence has become an effective tool for optimizing work schedules and reducing time loss. Proper organization of working hours with AI allows employees to maintain focus, improve performance, and avoid burnout caused by information overload and constant task switching.

Intelligent Planning and Time Allocation

AI-based scheduling systems analyze calendars, communication habits, and productivity patterns to recommend optimal task distribution. Applications such as Motion, Clockwise, or Microsoft 365 Copilot automatically form balanced schedules by identifying the best time for deep work, meetings, and recovery breaks.

This approach helps reduce decision fatigue — instead of manually organizing dozens of microtasks, employees can delegate these decisions to the system while keeping overall control.

Dynamic Adjustment During the Workday

Unlike traditional planners, AI assistants continuously adapt to real-time conditions. If a meeting is postponed or a new urgent task appears, the schedule is reorganized automatically. AI also detects time leaks caused by distractions, late responses, or excessive correspondence and offers specific corrections — for example, grouping short calls or summarizing unread emails.

Integration with Task Management Systems

When connected with platforms such as Asana, Trello, or Notion AI, assistants synchronize task lists and deadlines across different tools. This ensures that all updates remain consistent and visible to both the employee and the team. AI can also generate short daily briefings — compact summaries of goals and priorities — helping start each day with clarity.

Practical Implementation

To begin, it is advisable to entrust AI assistants with one function — for instance, daily scheduling or meeting coordination. After observing how the system adapts to your workflow, expand its responsibilities. Gradual integration allows for identifying the most effective settings without disrupting existing processes. Teams that apply this principle note a 10–20% reduction in unproductive time and a more even workload distribution throughout the week.

Key Advantages

- Reduced cognitive load through automated routine planning
- Flexible adjustment to changing priorities
- Improved concentration and fewer interruptions
- Transparent tracking of time use and workload balance

By combining analytical accuracy with adaptability, AI assistants transform time management into a predictable and measurable process. The employee retains control over goals and strategy while the system handles coordination, allowing human attention to remain where it brings the most value.

3.3 Tools for Project Management with AI Elements

Project management tools enhanced with artificial intelligence have evolved from simple planners into intelligent coordination systems. They now serve as analytical partners that help teams plan, predict, and adjust projects dynamically — not only tracking progress but learning from it. These systems combine automation, communication, and forecasting in one environment, reshaping how teams of any size organize their work.

Intelligent Planning and Resource Allocation

Modern AI tools such as Microsoft Copilot, ClickUp AI, Notion AI, and Asana Intelligence use natural language processing and predictive analytics to build adaptive project plans. They analyze timelines, workloads, and dependencies, then automatically generate task sequences and suggest resource allocation.

Unlike traditional scheduling, these assistants continuously recalculate priorities when new data arrives — such as changing deadlines, employee availability, or unexpected risks. Teams no longer spend hours in planning sessions; instead, they review AI-proposed timelines and confirm adjustments in seconds.

Smart Role Assignment and Workflow Automation

AI-powered platforms can analyze individual performance, skills, and focus time to distribute tasks objectively. For instance, Monday.com AI or Jira Advanced Roadmaps now integrate with internal analytics to determine who can best complete a given task, preventing overloads and improving fairness.

At the same time, built-in automation agents handle repetitive work — creating new tickets, updating task statuses, or sending reminders. This coordination ensures that human energy is reserved for analysis and creativity rather than administration.

Real-Time Monitoring and Risk Forecasting

AI now monitors project health in real time, interpreting large volumes of operational data. Dashboards powered by Power BI Copilot or Smartsheet AI automatically visualize trends, compare planned vs. actual performance, and flag early signs of delay or cost overrun.

Machine learning models identify risk factors — missed dependencies, recurring blockers, or inconsistent team velocity — and recommend preventive measures. For project leads, this means moving from reactive management to proactive decision-making based on evidence, not intuition.

Enhanced Communication and Collaboration

AI elements integrated into Slack GPT, Zoom AI Companion, and Google Workspace Duet AI streamline teamwork by summarizing discussions, assigning next steps, and maintaining shared context across platforms. Meeting notes, task briefs, and key insights are automatically synchronized with project dashboards, eliminating fragmentation.

Some tools even learn communication rhythms within teams, predicting optimal times for meetings or focus sessions and suggesting when asynchronous collaboration is more effective.

Predictive Analytics and Outcome Simulation

Modern systems apply deep learning to historical project data, allowing simulation of different strategic scenarios before they are executed. Managers can now model "what-if" outcomes — for example, how changing one milestone or reallocating one person might influence the overall timeline. This predictive insight reduces uncertainty and supports more informed decision-making.

Continuous Learning and Adaptability

AI project tools are self-improving. Over time, they refine their forecasts and suggestions as they accumulate data from each project cycle. This continuous adaptation makes the environment more personalized and precise, aligning with the team's evolving style and pace.

Application for Small and Medium Enterprises

While these technologies first appeared in large corporations, cloud-based platforms have made them accessible to small and medium businesses as well. Compact teams can use the same capabilities — automated scheduling, workload balancing, and performance tracking — without hiring a full-time project manager. For entrepreneurs, freelancers, and small offices, this means structured coordination at minimal cost.

Implementation and Employee Training

To integrate AI effectively, companies should start with gradual deployment — introducing automation in one area such as scheduling or reporting. Employees need short, practical training to understand not only how the system operates but why it improves efficiency.

The emerging role of an AI Project Coordinator or Workflow Integrator often becomes the bridge between human strategy and machine execution, ensuring that automation complements rather than replaces human judgment.

Practical Takeaways

- Begin with automation of repetitive administrative tasks.
- Use AI dashboards for early detection of risks and performance gaps.
- Encourage transparency: all participants should see how AI recommendations are formed.
- Provide training focused on understanding system logic and limits.

When used consciously, AI transforms project management from a sequence of tasks into an adaptive, self-optimizing process. Teams gain clarity, leaders gain foresight, and organizations gain a rhythm of steady, measurable improvement.

Chapter 4:
Ethics of using AI

4.1. Responsible use: where is the line between helping and replacing a person.

With the development of artificial intelligence (AI) technologies, an important question arises about the line between the help that this tool can provide to a person and its replacement in decision-making processes, performing tasks or interacting with other people. The use of AI in various fields, from medicine to finance and manufacturing, opens up new opportunities, but also presents us with difficult ethical challenges. This question is not only technical, but also deeply social, as it concerns how we, as a society, define the role of man in the conditions of rapidly developing technologies.

AI has enormous potential to improve the quality of life, make routine tasks easier, and even help make complex decisions. However, the question arises where the line should be drawn between the use of technology to support people and their replacement. After all, even the most advanced AI systems cannot completely replace the human capacity for empathy, moral judgment, and creativity, which remain unique human traits.

The responsible use of AI implies that technology should serve as a tool to improve efficiency and facilitate work, not to replace people at all stages of operations. It is important to realize that technology should be a tool that helps a person make better decisions, and not replace him in the process of making this decision. Given this, there is a need for a clear ethical framework to help define where AI assistance ends and its replacement begins.

One of the main aspects of the responsible use of AI is the recognition that, although AI is capable of many tasks, it does not possess human experience, intuition, or the capacity for moral judgment. This means that even in cases where AI can effectively perform routine or technical tasks, ethical decisions must be left to human discretion. For example, in medicine, AI can help in the analysis of medical images or in the prediction of diseases, but the final decision about treatment must be made by the doctor, who takes into account the individual circumstances of the patient.

This also applies to areas where AI can be used to automate work processes. For example, in manufacturing or in the service sector, AI can perform tasks that require high precision or speed, freeing people from routine work and giving them the opportunity to focus on more creative or strategic aspects. However, it is important that technology does not become the cause of a decrease in employment or social inequality, but on the contrary, contributes to the development of new opportunities for people, such as learning new skills or performing more responsible tasks.

Another important issue is security and privacy. AI is capable of processing large amounts of data, including personal information, which puts users' privacy and security at risk. The responsible use of AI requires that companies and organizations using these technologies adhere to high standards of security and privacy. This includes not only technical measures to protect data, but also an ethical approach to their use. It is important that people have control over their data and can choose which data is used to train AI models and which remains private.

At the same time, AI has the potential to help solve social problems, such as fighting poverty, improving access to education and healthcare. However, it is important to avoid situations where technology only exacerbates existing social inequalities. For example, automated systems that use AI to make credit or employment decisions may be biased if they are trained on data that contains historical stereotypes or discriminatory practices. This presents us with the task of developing such models that would ensure equality and justice in the processes where important decisions are made.

In the context of the responsible use of AI, it is also important to consider the impact of these technologies on culture and social relations. AI has the potential to change the way people interact with each other, particularly through automated communication systems such as chatbots or voice assistants. It is important that these technologies do not replace live communication, but complement it, allowing people to maintain their humanity and emotional connection.

The use of AI also requires us to constantly reflect on how these technologies change our understanding of work and human dignity. If we allow AI to replace humans in those areas where it is not only technically possible, but also economically beneficial, we risk losing not only jobs, but also important aspects of the social structure. Humans must remain at the center of technological change, and AI is only a tool that promotes the development of their capabilities, not a replacement for their role in society.

Therefore, the responsible use of AI is not only about creating technology that helps people, but also about defining the boundary where technology can complement the human, and where it must remain at the level of tools, not replacing the human role. It is important that in all areas of AI use we remember ethical principles based on respect for human dignity, privacy and social justice. Only then can technology become a real helper for a person, and not a replacement.

4.2. Issues of authorship and plagiarism when using AI.

With the development technologies of artificial intelligence, an important question arises: who is the author of what is created with the help of these technologies? The issue of authorship and plagiarism when using AI is becoming more and more relevant, since artificial intelligence is capable of generating texts, music, images and other creative works. This calls into question traditional ideas about who is the author of a work and how the results of AI work should be evaluated. At the same time, there is a need to develop clear ethical and legal standards that would help solve these issues.

AI as a tool for content creation can make the job much easier by speeding up the writing, editing and analysis processes. However, when it comes to authorship, the question arises: can a person be considered an author if the main part of the work was done by a machine? On the one hand, the user who uses AI to create texts or other works certainly has a large role in choosing the topic, setting the task and adjusting the results. However, on the other hand, the AI itself can do most of the work, creating content that sometimes feels completely autonomous.

Traditionally, authorship means recognition of a person's right to create a creative product that is the result of his intellectual work. However, in the case of AI, the situation is more complicated. If an AI generates text, music, or images based on human input, who owns the copyright? Is the author the person who set the parameters for the AI to work, or the AI itself that actually created the content? Or maybe the author is the AI developer, since he created the algorithms that allow these creations to be generated?

This question does not have an unequivocal answer. In many countries, copyright laws do not yet take into account the possibilities provided by AI. Traditionally, copyright is granted to the person who created the work, not to a machine or algorithm. However, when using AI to create content, it is difficult to determine who exactly is the author, as the human role in the creation process is often minimal. As a result, many lawyers and ethicists believe that it is necessary to revise existing legal norms to take into account the impact of new technologies.

One possible approach is to recognize as the author the person who exercises control over the content creation process, even if it uses AI. It can be a human who chooses parameters, provides input, and determines the direction of the AI. This approach preserves the traditional understanding of authorship, while recognizing the important role of technology in creating a result. However, this approach also begs the question of whether it is fair to credit a human as the author who merely points the way, while the AI is actually doing most of the work.

Another approach is to consider the result of AI work as a joint work, where the role of man and machine is equal. In this case, both the human and the AI will be considered the author, and the rights to the work will be shared between them. This allows for a more accurate representation of the interaction between humans and technology, but also raises new questions about how to allocate rights to works created with AI.

Another important aspect is the issue of plagiarism when using AI. Because AI is able to generate content based on large amounts of data, there is a risk that a machine can create works that are similar to existing works without proper acknowledgment of the authorship of the original works. This can lead to situations where AI-generated content is considered plagiarism, even if the user had no intention of infringing copyright. It is important that AI users are aware of the risks of plagiarism and use technology responsibly to avoid infringing the rights of other authors.

In this regard, there is a need to develop new ethical norms that would regulate the use of AI for content creation. One of the possible solutions is to create clear rules that would define exactly what constitutes permissible use of AI and what constitutes copyright infringement. This could include requiring AI users to clearly state that their content was generated using the technology, and to give proper credit to the original authors if their work was used in the generation process.

It is also important that AI developers consider ethical aspects when creating their technologies. For example, they can implement mechanisms that allow determining whether the content created is original or contains elements that violate copyright. This can help reduce the risk of plagiarism and ensure a more ethical use of AI in creative processes.

In general, the issue of authorship and plagiarism in the use of AI is complex and requires further research and the development of new ethical and legal norms. It is important that technology not only helps people create new works, but also ensures that the rights to these works are distributed fairly and that the rights of the original authors are protected.

4.3. Transparency: How to tell customers and colleagues about the use of AI.

Transparency in the use of artificial intelligence technologies is one of the main ethical issues facing both businesses and their employees and customers. An important part of this transparency is reporting exactly how AI is used in processes related to both internal company operations and customer interactions. Explaining the principles of using AI helps build trust, avoid misunderstandings, and even protect the company from potential legal issues.

Whether AI is being used to automate internal processes, analyze data, generate content or interact with customers, it is important to clearly communicate this to all stakeholders. Customers and colleagues need to understand when and why AI is used, and what results to expect from it. This not only increases the level of trust, but also avoids situations where the technology can be perceived as something opaque or even hidden.

The importance of transparency is that AI can change the way decisions are made. If a person or organization does not communicate the use of AI, it can lead to mistrust or even assumptions that decisions are made without adequate human input. Customers may feel that their interests are not taken into account, and employees may feel that their role in decision-making is diminished. That's why it's important to be clear about how and why AI is being used to maintain trust and understanding.

Educating clients about the use of AI can be difficult, as many may not be familiar with the technology or understand its impact on business outcomes. Therefore, it is important to explain it in simple and accessible language. For example, if a company uses AI to analyze data about customer purchases in order to provide personalized recommendations, this should be explained, emphasizing that this is done to improve the customer experience. It is important to point out that such recommendations are not the result of random or unpredictable actions, but the result of algorithms that analyze the data received from the client.

Transparency also includes discussing exactly how customer data is used and stored. Modern AI technologies often require large amounts of data to work effectively. Therefore, issues of privacy and data security become important aspects of transparency. Customers must be confident that their data is not being used without their permission and that it is protected from unauthorized access. Explaining the privacy policy and data processing methods helps create a sense of safety and security among users.

In addition, it is important to understand that the use of AI can be not only a technological issue, but also an ethical one. For example, AI can make decisions that affect people, such as granting loans or making employment decisions. In such cases, companies should clearly communicate exactly how AI is involved in decision-making and why it is important to the customer or employee. If AI decisions lead to a loan rejection or reduced employment chances, it is necessary to explain how this process works and whether there is an opportunity to appeal the decision made by the machine.

As for colleagues, transparency should also be a key principle in the interaction between employees and management. The internal use of AI in the company must be clear to all employees so that they can adapt to changes and interact effectively with new technologies. When employees understand exactly how AI is used in their work, it reduces the stress and uncertainty that comes with new technologies and allows them to better integrate these technologies into their daily tasks.

In addition, management should ensure that employees have the opportunity to receive feedback on the use of AI and its impact on their work. This may include regular trainings or meetings where employees can express their comments and suggestions regarding the use of AI. Transparency also means that employees have a clear understanding of how their role is changing as new technologies are introduced. If AI automates certain aspects of work, it is important that employees are aware of this in advance and have the opportunity to adapt their skills and tasks to the new conditions.

At the same time, transparency does not mean that every stage of working with AI should be open to everyone. In some cases, it may be necessary to maintain some confidentiality, especially when it comes to commercial strategies or personal data. However, even in such cases, it is important that there are clear boundaries and rules regarding what can and cannot be disclosed. This will help avoid misunderstandings and maintain a balance between transparency and privacy.

In general, transparency in the use of AI is an important ethical principle that allows maintaining trust between a company and its customers, as well as between management and employees. Informing about the use of AI helps to avoid misunderstandings, ensures the effective integration of new technologies and allows to create an atmosphere of openness and cooperation. It is important to remember that transparency should not only be in words, but also in action, which allows you to build strong and trusting relationships with all interested parties.

Chapter 5:

Data security when working with AI

5.1. How AI processes your data: myths and reality.

Technologies of artificial intelligence (AI) are becoming more and more integrated into our everyday processes, the issue of data security is gaining particular importance. You may have heard a lot of myths about how AI processes your data and how it can affect your privacy. However, it is important to understand that not all of these ideas correspond to reality. In this section, we will look at the most common myths and facts about data processing with AI, so that you can better understand how these technologies work and why it is important to approach the issue of security correctly.

One of the most common myths is that AI collects all the data about users without their knowledge and consent. In fact, it is not quite so. Although AI requires large amounts of data to work effectively, modern technologies require clear rules and protocols for collecting, storing and processing this data. Most companies that use AI have privacy policies that govern how data is collected and used. They also often give users the ability to control what data is collected and what is not. In addition, it is important to remember that data collection usually occurs within well-defined purposes, such as improving a product or service.

Another common myth is the notion that AI can collect all of a user's personal data and use it for manipulation or malicious purposes. This is not so. Although AI can process large amounts of information, it does not have "consciousness" or "intentions" as it is often imagined in popular movies or books. AI works on the basis of algorithms that determine exactly how to process data, but these algorithms are not capable of making decisions on their own. They only perform tasks assigned to them by programmers or users. Most of today's AI systems are limited to certain frameworks to avoid abuse or misuse of data.

You can also often hear that all the data that is collected through AI can be easily studied and used by third parties. This is also a myth, as most modern technologies provide different levels of data protection. AI systems often use encryption and other security methods to ensure that information is protected from unauthorized access. For example, when processing personal data, it is important to ensure anonymity, so that even in the event of a data leak, the user's identity remains protected.

One important aspect to consider is data storage. Many people believe that all data collected by AI is stored indefinitely and can be used in the future without permission. In fact, most companies have clear data retention policies that define how long information can be kept, when it should be deleted, and how to ensure that it is protected during that period. This is important not only from a security perspective, but also to comply with legislation that regulates the processing of personal data, such as the General Data Protection Regulation (GDPR) in the European Union.

One of the biggest fears surrounding the use of AI is the potential for unauthorized access to data. This issue becomes even more relevant when it comes to processing sensitive information such as financial data or medical records. However, it is important to understand that companies that work with such data usually use additional layers of protection. For example, in the financial sector, special algorithms are used to detect fraud, and in the medical sector, patient data is often stored in encrypted form, making it inaccessible to outsiders.

In fact, AI can help significantly improve data security. For example, AI can be used to create systems that can automatically detect anomalies in large amounts of data that may indicate attempts at unauthorized access or fraud. Such systems can work much faster and more efficiently than traditional methods, allowing timely detection of threats and reducing the risk of data leaks.

Another myth that often comes up in the context of data security is that AI is so complex that it cannot be controlled or regulated. This is not quite so. Although AI technologies are indeed developing rapidly, there are clear mechanisms to control them. Legislatures around the world are developing regulations that govern the use of AI, particularly in the context of data security. For example, in the European Union there are legislative initiatives aimed at creating ethical standards for the use of AI, which includes mandatory requirements for the protection of personal data.

One important aspect of data security when using AI is the need for employee training and awareness. AI technologies are often used not only to automate processes, but also to analyze large volumes of data, which requires a high level of competence from those who work with these systems. Companies must ensure that their employees are trained to understand how AI systems work, what risks exist, and how these risks can be minimized.

At the same time, it is important to note that while AI can provide a high level of data security, it is not a panacea for all problems. AI technologies have their limitations, and even the most advanced systems can be vulnerable to new types of attacks or failures. Therefore, it is important to use AI in conjunction with other data protection methods, such as physical security, regular software updates, and other strategies that allow for a comprehensive approach to security.

In general, understanding how AI processes your data helps dispel many myths and reduce fears associated with this technology. While AI does have enormous potential to improve safety and efficiency, it is important to remember that its use must be controlled and ethical. Correct understanding and transparency in the issue of data processing help to maintain the trust of users and ensure reliable protection of their personal data.

5.2. Security Best Practices: Avoiding Information Leaks.

In the context of the integration of artificial intelligence (AI) into various spheres of activity, in particular at workplaces, the protection of confidential information becomes critically important. Data leakage can lead not only to financial losses, but also to loss of customer trust, reputational losses and legal consequences. Therefore, it is important to understand how AI systems work with data and what steps can be taken to minimize the risks of information leakage.

The main problem is that many people do not understand exactly how their data is processed when interacting with AI. This may be due to the underestimation of potential threats or the blocking of technologies used to protect them. Therefore, the first step to security is to understand how data enters the AI system and how it can be used.

AI works with data, processing it to train models, make decisions, or automate processes. This data can include personal information, financial data, professional habits and even behavioral patterns. It is important to understand that the data that enters the AI system can be stored, processed and even used to create new products or services. However, if this data is not properly protected, it can be extracted from the system by attackers or fall into the hands of unauthorized persons.

The first step to preventing information leakage is to ensure that data access is properly controlled. This includes using strong passwords, multi-factor authentication, and regularly updating passwords and controlling access rights to systems. It is important to limit access to sensitive data only to those employees who have a direct relationship with it. This reduces the probability of unauthorized access and the possibility of data leakage due to the human factor.

In addition, it is necessary to apply data encryption. Encryption is one of the most effective ways to protect information, especially when it is transmitted over a network. Encryption can be used to transform data into an unrecognizable form, making it inaccessible to those who do not have the decryption key. It is important that encryption is applied not only to the data that is stored, but also to that which is transmitted over the Internet or other communication channels.

One of the important aspects of security when working with AI is the use of reliable platforms and systems. If a company uses third-party services for data processing or AI integration, it is important to ensure that these platforms meet high security standards. This includes checking for security certifications such as ISO 27001, as well as regular security audits to identify possible vulnerabilities in the system.

Training the company's employees in the basics of data security is also an important aspect. Information leaks often occur due to human error or negligence. Employees must understand what data is confidential, how it is handled and stored, and what actions could lead to a security breach. Regular cyber security training and employee knowledge testing can significantly reduce the risk of information leakage.

Another important step is the monitoring and auditing of AI systems. Continuous monitoring of systems allows you to detect abnormal actions or attempts of unauthorized access to data. If a potential threat is identified, the company can promptly take measures to neutralize the risk. It is important that this process is automated, as it allows threats to be detected at an early stage, before they can lead to serious consequences.

Data protection also involves proper storage and deletion of information. Once data is no longer needed to process or train AI models, it must be securely deleted. This is important to prevent information leakage through old or unused systems. Data deletion should be carried out using special tools that ensure that the information cannot be recovered after its destruction.

One of the new approaches to security is the use of blockchain technology for data storage. Blockchain allows you to create a decentralized database where every change is recorded in the system and cannot be changed without a corresponding record. This makes the data more secure against unauthorized access or modification. The use of blockchain can be an important element in improving data security in AI systems, especially in areas such as financial services or healthcare.

An equally important aspect is ensuring the transparency of data processing processes. Users and customers must have a clear understanding of what data is collected, how it is processed and stored, and who has access to it. This allows you to build trust in

AI systems and reduces the risk of legal consequences in the event of a data leak. Companies must publish privacy policies and inform their customers about how their data is used.

Data protection in AI work also includes constant software updates. System and program updates help close vulnerabilities that can be used by attackers to gain access to data. This is important to ensure that AI systems are always running on the latest versions of software that contain the latest security features.

Finally, it is important to consider the ethical aspects of working with data. Since AI can process huge amounts of information, ethical principles must be considered when making decisions related to the use of this data. For example, companies must avoid discriminating against or violating users' rights by using algorithms that do not violate their rights or lead to undesirable consequences.

Therefore, data security when working with AI is a complex problem that requires an integrated approach that includes both technical and organizational measures. It is important to be aware of the risks associated with data processing and take appropriate measures to minimize them.

5.3. Tools with a high level of confidentiality.

Artificial intelligence (AI) is increasingly penetrating various spheres of activity, the issue of data privacy is gaining particular importance. This is especially true for organizations that work with sensitive information, where even the smallest data leak can lead to serious consequences. Tools that provide a high level of privacy are necessary to ensure data security when using AI. They help reduce the risks associated with the processing and storage of information containing personal or corporate secrets.

Using such tools not only helps keep information secure, but also ensures that organizations can comply with regulatory requirements such as the General Data Protection Regulation (GDPR) in the European Union or the California Consumer Privacy Protection Act (CCPA) in the US. These laws set clear requirements for the processing of personal data, and breaching these requirements can result in heavy fines and reputational damage.

One of the main tools that ensure a high level of privacy is data encryption. Encryption converts information into a format that cannot be read without a special key. This method allows you to protect data even if an attacker gains access to it. There are different types of encryption, and the choice depends on the specific needs of the organization. For example, disk-level encryption allows you to protect all information stored on a computer or server, while file-level encryption allows you to protect individual documents.

Another important tool is multi-factor authentication (MFA). It provides an additional layer of protection by requiring the user not only to enter a password, but also to verify their identity using additional factors, such as a code sent to a mobile phone, or biometric data such as fingerprints or facial recognition. MFA greatly reduces the chance of unauthorized access to the system, even if an attacker gets hold of the user's password.

Data Loss Prevention (DLP) tools are another important component of a security strategy. They allow you to monitor and control data transmission over the network, detecting attempts at unauthorized access or transmission of sensitive information. Such systems can be configured to automatically block the transmission of certain types of data or to warn the user that they are attempting to transmit sensitive information.

For working with AI, it is also important to use tools that allow you to control access to data. These can be access management systems (IAM, Identity and Access Management), which allow you to determine who and what data can be viewed or edited. They help limit access to sensitive information to only those employees who have the appropriate rights to do so. In addition, these systems can keep an access log that allows you to track who accessed the data and when, which is important for identifying potential threats.

Also an important aspect is the use of technologies for anonymization and pseudonymization of data. These methods allow you to hide identification data, reducing the risks of personal information leakage. Anonymization involves the complete removal of all identifying data, which makes it impossible to restore personal information. Pseudonymization, in turn, replaces identifying data with pseudonyms, which allows you to preserve the usefulness of data for analytics, while reducing the risks of leakage.

Other tools that can help ensure data privacy include a variety of security monitoring systems that can detect anomalous activity in real time. They can help detect unauthorized access attempts or other threats, allowing you to quickly respond to security incidents.

Data protection when working with AI also involves the use of risk management tools. These can be software tools for assessing vulnerabilities, which allow you to identify weak points in systems and take measures to eliminate them in time. Such tools allow for regular security checks, ensuring timely detection of new threats.

And ultimately, it's important to understand that even the best security tools can't guarantee absolute security if employees aren't properly trained. The human factor is one of the main causes of data leaks, so regular security training and raising employee awareness about the proper handling of confidential information is an important part of a security strategy.

Using tools with a high level of privacy is a necessary step to ensure data security when working with AI. They help protect sensitive information from leaks and unauthorized access, reducing risks for organizations and their customers. However, it is important to remember that in order to achieve the maximum level of security, these tools must be used in conjunction with other measures, such as employee training, regular software updates and constant security monitoring.

Chapter 6:

The Future of AI at Work

6.1. How AI is changing professions: prospects for development.

Artificial intelligence (AI) is already changing many professions and industries, and these changes will only intensify in the future. With the development of technology, AI is becoming more and more integrated into work processes, changing approaches to performing tasks, as well as creating new opportunities and challenges for employees. It is important to understand exactly how these changes affect the professions that already exist, as well as what new professions are emerging due to the introduction of AI.

One of the most obvious impacts of AI is the automation of routine and repetitive tasks. This applies to many occupations, from production workers to office workers. AI can automate many processes such as data entry, document processing, inventory management, even certain steps in customer service processes. For example, chatbots and virtual assistants can handle customer inquiries by providing answers to frequently asked questions, allowing employees to focus on more complex tasks.

On the other hand, AI not only replaces humans in performing routine tasks, but also creates new opportunities for professions that did not exist before. From the emergence of new roles such as AI engineers, data analysts, algorithm developers, to new areas of work such as AI ethics, data protection, and even experts in managing the impact of technology on society.

Careers related to AI require knowledge in the fields of programming, mathematics, statistics, and a deep understanding of the ethics and social aspects of technology.

AI is also changing the nature of work in fields such as medicine, education, finance and marketing. For example, in medicine, AI helps doctors make diagnoses faster and more accurately by analyzing large volumes of medical data, such as images from MRIs or X-rays. This allows to reduce the probability of errors and improve the effectiveness of treatment. In the field of education, AI can personalize learning by creating individualized programs for each student that take into account their learning pace and learning style.

At the same time, in the financial field, AI is already actively used to predict market trends, automate trading, and even fight fraud. Thanks to machine learning algorithms, systems can detect anomalies in financial transactions and warn of possible violations in a timely manner. In marketing, AI is used to analyze big data, which allows you to create personalized advertising campaigns, focusing on the interests and behavior of consumers.

However, with the development of AI, new challenges for employees arise. They must adapt to new conditions, which involve changing approaches to work, as well as the need for constant training and professional development. It is important to understand that AI is not just replacing people, but rather changing the very nature of work. Workers must learn to use AI as a tool to improve their work efficiency, not as a threat.

So, for example, in the field of jurisprudence, AI can help lawyers analyze large volumes of legal documents, which significantly reduces the time spent on preparing cases. However, at the same time, lawyers must remain responsible for making final decisions, since AI cannot completely replace human intuition and the ability to assess situations in the context of specific cases.

An equally important aspect is the change in the role of managers. Technologies that allow automation of management processes change the requirements for leaders. They must be ready to use the latest tools to optimize business processes and make decisions based on data. However, even though AI can help with decision-making, strategic thinking, people management and emotional intelligence remain important skills for managers.

The changes taking place affect not only professions, but also the working environment itself. AI allows creating new forms of collaboration, for example, in the form of hybrid teams where people work alongside artificial intelligence. This maximizes the benefits of both parties: humans can apply their creative and analytical skills, while AI performs computational tasks and helps in decision-making. This model of collaboration requires employees to develop new skills, such as the ability to collaborate with technology, adaptability and readiness for change.

In the future, we can expect AI to become an integral part of most professions. This does not mean that humans will be replaced by machines, but the role of humans in many areas will change. Technology will help people focus on more important aspects of work, such as creativity, strategic thinking and interaction with other people, while routine and monotonous tasks will be automated.

The professionals of the future must be prepared for the fact that knowledge of technology and the ability to work with AI will become mandatory. They must be able to effectively use the tools provided by AI to improve their productivity and achieve better results in their work. Education and continuous learning will be key elements for those who want to remain competitive in the labor market.

Thus, AI is already changing professions, but these changes are just beginning. A future in which AI helps people do their jobs more efficiently and accurately is just around the corner. The main thing is to be ready for these changes and to be able to adapt to new conditions.

6.2. Skills worth developing to stay competitive.

In today's realities, it is important not only to monitor the development of technologies, but also to understand which skills will allow you to remain competitive in the labor market. AI not only changes the way work is done, but also creates new demands on workers, forcing them to adapt to new realities. Therefore, it is important not only to learn new tools, but also to develop skills that allow you to work effectively in the conditions of technological changes.

One of the key skills that must be developed in the context of the development of AI is the ability to constantly learn. The rapid development of technologies requires employees to constantly update their knowledge. What was relevant a few years ago may no longer meet the requirements of the modern market. The ability to quickly master new tools and technologies, particularly those related to AI, will be an important competitive advantage. This doesn't mean you need to know every aspect of AI, but having a basic understanding of the field will give you a better understanding of how to use technology to improve your own work.

In addition, one of the important skills is the ability to think creatively. Although AI can automate many routine tasks, it cannot yet replace human creativity. The development of creative skills will allow finding non-standard solutions, creating new ideas and approaches to solving problems. This is especially important in areas such as marketing, design, advertising, where creativity is the basis of success. Technology can help with data analysis, but it is humans who can generate innovative ideas that respond to consumer and market needs.

Communication skills are also of particular importance in the context of the development of AI. Given that many tasks will be automated, the need for effective communication with other people is increasing. Cooperation with colleagues, the ability to conduct negotiations, the ability to work in a team and effectively present ideas become important success factors. In an environment where part of the work is done by AI, the ability to communicate clearly and lead becomes even more important.

Another important skill is emotional intelligence. Since AI cannot completely replace human perception of emotions and social interactions, the ability to understand and effectively interact with people will be one of the most important competencies. Emotional intelligence includes the ability to recognize other people's emotions, manage one's own emotions, and create a favorable atmosphere for cooperation and interaction. This is especially important in those professions that require working with people, such as customer service, management and consulting.

The ability to work with data is also becoming a necessary skill for the modern worker. AI is capable of processing large amounts of information, but a person must be able to correctly interpret this data and use it to make informed decisions. Knowledge of the basics of statistics, data analysis and the ability to work with information processing tools allow you to obtain useful conclusions from data that can be used to optimize business processes, improve products or services. In addition, being able to work with data allows you to understand how AI processes information and how you can use these capabilities to improve your own work.

No less important is the ability to adapt. AI and technology in general are evolving very quickly, and employees need to be ready for change. Adaptability means the ability to quickly respond to new conditions, learn on the go and change your approaches to work. This is important not only in the context of new technologies, but also in connection with changes in work processes, in organizational structures and in business models. Workers who can quickly adapt to new conditions will have significantly greater competitiveness in the labor market.

In addition, understanding the ethics of technology is an important aspect. As AI becomes more integrated into various aspects of life, it is important to understand the ethical issues that arise in connection with its use. How to ensure data privacy? How to avoid bias in algorithms? How to ensure transparency and fairness in the use of AI? The answers to these questions become important for all workers, especially those who work with technology or in fields where the use of AI can have serious social consequences. Understanding the ethics of technology and the ability to take it into account at work will allow employees to be not only technically savvy, but also socially responsible.

Critical thinking and analytical skills are other important skills. Although AI can perform many tasks with high accuracy, it cannot always assess the situation in context or take into account all possible scenarios. A person must be able to critically evaluate the results provided by AI and make decisions based on this analysis. This allows you to avoid mistakes and make more informed decisions, even when technology does not provide clear answers.

Project management and leadership skills also remain important as AI becomes an important part of the workflow. Leaders must be able to organize teams, including both people and technology, to achieve the best results. The ability to work with teams, motivate them, and ensure effective collaboration between humans and AI is becoming a key factor for success in many fields.

Therefore, in order to remain competitive in a world where AI plays an increasingly important role, it is necessary to develop a whole range of skills. The ability to constantly learn, think creatively, communicate effectively, work with data, adapt to changes, and understand the ethical issues of technology are the skills that will help employees not only maintain their competitiveness, but also succeed in new conditions.

6.3. How to adapt to rapid changes in technology.

Adapting to rapid changes in technology is one of the most important components of success in an environment where artificial intelligence and other technologies are rapidly changing the landscape of work processes. Every year, new innovations come to the market at such a speed that many workers cannot keep up with them. Technologies that seemed fantastic just a few years ago are now commonplace tools used in various industries. Therefore, it is important to understand how to adapt to these changes and how to remain competitive in a world where technology is changing rapidly.

The first step to adaptation is understanding that change is inevitable. In a world where new technologies appear all the time, it is important to change your attitude towards change. Many people feel afraid or anxious about new technologies because they can seem complicated and confusing. However, if you consider technology as an opportunity for development, and not as a threat, it will allow you to more easily perceive changes and look for new opportunities in them. Understanding that change is not something to be afraid of, but part of a normal development process, will help you stay calm and focus on how to use new tools to improve your work.

The second important aspect of adaptation is readiness for continuous learning. The speed of technology development is such that even the best professionals must constantly update their knowledge to keep up with the market. The ability to quickly learn new tools and technologies is not just an advantage, but a necessity for every employee. However, learning doesn't have to be a complicated or lengthy process. Many modern learning platforms offer courses and resources that allow you to learn new technologies in a short time. It is also important to learn not only the technical aspects, but also to understand how these technologies can be used to improve work and achieve specific results.

In addition, adaptation to technological change requires the development of flexibility and the ability to quickly change approaches. If earlier it was possible to work according to a certain plan for a long time, now you need to be ready to change strategies, approaches and methods of work depending on new conditions. This applies not only to technology, but also to changes in the market, employee requirements and business processes. Flexibility allows you to quickly respond to new challenges and adapt your skills and strategies according to the situation. In such conditions, it is important not only to know how to work with new technologies, but also how to quickly find new opportunities to improve processes and results.

Developing critical thinking skills is also an important part of adaptation. Although technology can help automate many tasks, it cannot always replace the human ability to analyze and assess a situation. AI and other technologies can provide a huge amount of data, but it is important to be able to interpret it correctly and use it to make decisions. Critical thinking allows you to evaluate the results that technology provides and make more informed decisions, even if those results are not completely accurate or unambiguous.

Another important aspect is the ability to work in conditions of uncertainty. In a world where technology is constantly changing, it is difficult to predict which tools and methods will be relevant in a few years. Therefore, it is important to be able to work in conditions where information is constantly updated, and decisions are made based on data that can change. The ability to work in such conditions allows you to maintain efficiency and not lose your bearings, even when the situation looks unstable.

For successful adaptation, it is also important to be open to new ideas and approaches. Sometimes people resist change because they are used to certain ways of working or they are afraid of losing control over the process. However, being open to new ideas allows you not only to adapt to change, but also to use it to your advantage. Technologies that may seem complex or confusing can become powerful tools for improving work if approached with an open mind and a willingness to experiment.

Equally important is the development of effective communication skills. In a world where technology is constantly changing, it is important to be able to clearly and clearly explain your ideas, as well as to interact effectively with other people. Communication with colleagues, partners and clients is key to success in any field. The ability to explain complex technological aspects in an accessible language allows not only to avoid misunderstandings, but also to find a common language with people who do not have deep knowledge in certain fields.

In general, adapting to rapid changes in technology requires employees to be flexible, willing to learn and develop new skills. The ability to quickly master new tools, work in conditions of uncertainty and communicate effectively with other people allows not only to remain competitive, but also to use technology to achieve better results. Constantly changing technologies can be a powerful tool for development if approached with openness and readiness for change.

Appendices

Glossary of AI terms.

Artificial intelligence (AI) is one of the most rapidly developing technologies that permeates all spheres of life. From business to healthcare, from science to everyday life — AI is changing approaches to problem solving and creating new opportunities. However, due to its complexity and specificity, many terms related to AI can be confusing to those who do not work directly with the technology. Therefore, it is important to have a clear understanding of the basic terms in order to be able to work effectively with AI and use its potential in your professional activities.

Algorithm is a set of instructions or rules that determine how to perform a task or solve a problem. In the context of AI, algorithms are used to train models that can then make predictions or make decisions based on input data.

Machine Learning (ML) is a subfield of AI that allows computers to learn from data without explicit programming. Machine learning uses statistical techniques to find patterns and patterns in large amounts of data, allowing for predictions or decision making.

Deep learning (Deep Learning) is a subfield of machine learning that uses multi-layer neural networks to automatically learn from large amounts of data. Deep learning is used to solve complex problems such as image recognition, natural language processing and autonomous driving.

Neural network is a mathematical model inspired by the work of the human brain, which consists of neurons (nodes) connected to each other. Neural networks are used in deep learning to solve complex problems such as pattern recognition, language or prediction.

Natural language (Natural Language Processing, NLP) is a subfield of AI that deals with the interaction between computers and human language. NLP allows machines to understand, interpret, and generate text or language in a human-like way.

Computer vision (Computer Vision) is a branch of AI that allows computers to "see" and interpret images or videos. Computer vision technologies are used to recognize objects, persons, texts, as well as to analyze and process visual information.

Autonomous systems are systems capable of making decisions and performing tasks without human intervention. An example of such systems are autonomous cars that are able to move and orient themselves on the road without the intervention of the driver.

Artificial neural network (Artificial Neural Network, ANN) is a type of neural network used to model complex functions and decisions based on learning from data. An ANN consists of several layers of neurons through which data passes, and each layer is responsible for certain information processing.

Convolutional Neural Networks (CNN) is a type of neural network that is particularly effective for image and video processing. CNNs are capable of automatically detecting important features in images, such as edges, textures, or objects, making them ideal for computer vision tasks.

Recurrent Neural Networks (RNN) is a type of neural network that specializes in processing sequential data such as text, audio, or video. RNNs use previous states to process current data, allowing them to preserve context and make predictions based on sequences.

Model training is the process in which a machine learning model is trained on data. Training consists of tuning the parameters of a model so that it can make accurate predictions or classifications on new, unknown data.

Overfitting is a situation where a machine learning model fits the training data too well and begins to perform poorly on new data. This is because the model remembers specific details of the training data, rather than learning to find general patterns.

Underfitting is a situation where the model is unable to capture important patterns in the data and does not perform well even on the training data.

Model parameters are values that are adjusted during model training so that it can perform its functions correctly. The parameters determine how the model processes the input data and makes predictions.

Model testing is the stage where the model is tested against new, unknown data to assess its accuracy and effectiveness. This allows you to understand how well the model will work in real conditions.

Generative models is a type of machine learning model that is capable of generating new data similar to the data it was trained on. An example of such models are generative adversarial networks (GANs), which are used to generate fake images, texts or videos.

Interpretability of the model is the ability to understand how the model makes its decisions. Interpretability is important for understanding why a model makes certain predictions or classifications, which is especially important in fields such as medicine or finance.

Artificial intelligence with limitations (Weak AI) is a type of AI that can perform specific tasks but lacks general intelligence or consciousness. It cannot perform tasks that were not foreseen by the programmers.

Artificial General Intelligence (AGI, Artificial General Intelligence) is a type of AI that has the ability to perform any task that a human can perform. This is a more complex and powerful level of AI that has not yet been achieved, but is the goal of many researchers.

Intelligent agents are programs or systems that can perform automatic actions in a certain environment, observing it and reacting to changes. Intelligent agents can be used to automate various processes, from recommendations to resource management.

Robotics is a branch of engineering and technology that deals with the development of robots that can perform physical tasks. Artificial intelligence is often integrated into robots so that they can make decisions and adapt to changing conditions.

Ethics is a branch of ethics that examines moral issues related to the use of AI. This includes issues of privacy, security, accountability for decisions made by machines, and possible consequences for society.

Big Data is a term that refers to huge amounts of data that are extremely difficult to process using traditional methods. AI and machine learning are used to analyze and extract useful information from such data.

Internet of Things (IoT, Internet of Things) is a concept that involves connecting different devices to the Internet to exchange data. AI can be used to analyze the data received from these devices to improve efficiency and automate processes.

This glossary is only a basic set of terms encountered by AI professionals and workers. It is important to remember that technology is constantly evolving, and every year new terms and concepts appear that can help unlock the potential of AI and its applications in various areas of life.

List of popular tools and platforms with short descriptions.

There are many tools and platforms that help both large corporations and small businesses integrate the latest technologies into their operations. These tools can help automate processes, improve operational efficiency, reduce costs, and improve decision-making accuracy. Here are some popular platforms and tools that have become mainstream in AI work.

First of all, one of the most famous platforms is **TensorFlow**. It is an open source tool developed by Google that allows you to create, train and implement machine learning models. TensorFlow is a versatile tool that supports a wide range of tasks, from image processing to natural language processing. Its popularity is due to its power and flexibility, as well as a large number of libraries and support for various programming languages, which allows it to be easily integrated into various projects.

PyTorch is another powerful machine learning tool developed by Facebook. PyTorch is popular for its convenience for researchers and developers. This tool has a feature of a dynamic calculation graph, which allows the model to change during training, which greatly facilitates testing and modification. PyTorch is actively used to create models related to computer vision and text processing.

Another popular platform is **Microsoft Azure AI**, which offers a set of tools for building, training and implementing AI models. The platform supports various types of machine learning, and also includes tools for working with big data, automating business processes, and creating chatbots. Azure AI allows companies to easily integrate AI into their systems without having to develop complex algorithms themselves.

IBM Watson is another platform that allows you to use AI to automate processes, analyze data, and make decisions. Watson offers a variety of tools for working with text, images, language, and even for creating chatbots. This tool is widely used in healthcare, finance and legal services to automate data processing and decision making.

Google Cloud AI is a set of tools that allow users to create, train, and implement AI models on Google's infrastructure. Google Cloud AI offers solutions for processing text, images, video and audio, and also supports the automation of business processes and the creation of personalized recommendations. One of the main advantages of this platform is its scalability and ability to work with large amounts of data.

An equally important tool is **H2O.ai**, which specializes in building models for machine learning and deep learning. This platform allows you to build models for prediction, classification, clustering and other tasks based on data. H2O.ai also has an interface that allows you to work with data without the need for deep programming knowledge, making it accessible to business users.

For those working with natural language processing, **spaCy** is a powerful tool for creating models that work with texts. This library supports a wide range of tasks such as text analysis, entity recognition, text classification and much more. spaCy is a fast and efficient tool that allows developers to quickly build and test natural language processing models.

RapidMiner is another tool that allows you to perform data analysis, create machine learning models and implement them in real business processes. RapidMiner is convenient for users with no programming experience because it provides a graphical interface for creating models, which allows you to focus on solving business problems without the need to write code.

Great for working with data and building models based on big data **Databricks**. This platform supports work with Apache Spark, which allows you to process huge amounts of data, and also provides tools for machine learning and creating analytical models. Databricks are actively used by large companies to process data in real time and to create scalable models.

Another popular tool is **Hard**, which is a high-level library for creating neural networks. Keras is part of TensorFlow, but can also work with other platforms such as Theano or Microsoft Cognitive Toolkit. This tool allows developers to quickly build deep learning models with a simple and easy-to-understand API.

Painting is a data visualization platform that is heavily used for data analysis and interactive reporting. It allows you to integrate AI into data analysis processes, giving users the opportunity to visualize the results of the models and obtain useful business insights based on them.

Chatbot tools are also essential for automating customer interactions. One such tool is **Dialog Flow**, developed by Google. This platform allows you to create smart chatbots that can conduct dialogues with users in different languages and integrate with different communication channels, such as messengers, websites and even voice assistants.

It is actively used to automate marketing and personalize content **HubSpot**, which provides tools for analyzing user behavior, automating communications and creating personalized recommendations. The AI in this platform helps businesses increase the effectiveness of marketing campaigns and improve customer interactions.

Another popular tool for working with data is **Alteryx**, which allows you to perform deep data analysis and create analytical models without the need for programming. Alteryx provides powerful tools for data processing, data visualization and integration with other decision-making platforms.

In addition, it is worth mentioning about **Scikit-learn**, a popular Python machine learning library that provides tools for classification, regression, clustering, and other tasks. Scikit-learn is one of the most used libraries in academia and business for building data-driven models.

Amazon Web Services (AWS) also provides powerful AI tools such as **AWS SageMaker**, which allows you to create, train and deploy machine learning models. AWS supports a wide range of tasks, from working with big data to creating recommender systems and automating business processes.

These tools and platforms are just part of the vast array of opportunities open to companies looking to integrate AI into their business processes. Each of these tools has its own advantages and characteristics, and the choice depends on the specific needs of the business and the level of training of the users. It is important to consider not only technical characteristics, but also ease of use, community support and the possibility of integration with other systems.

Learning Resources for AI in the Workplace

For those seeking to deepen their knowledge of artificial intelligence (AI) and its practical applications at work, a variety of high-quality resources are available. These include online courses, books, tutorials, research platforms, and professional communities that cover both theoretical concepts and hands-on skills. Leveraging these resources can enhance your understanding of AI, improve your workflow, and help you stay current with emerging technologies.

Online courses and educational platforms are among the most accessible ways to build knowledge. Coursera offers a wide range of AI courses, from introductory topics to specialized areas such as machine learning, natural language processing, computer vision, and generative AI applications. Courses are designed by leading universities and companies, including Stanford, MIT, and Google, providing both theoretical grounding and practical exercises.

Similarly, **edX** hosts courses from institutions like Harvard and Microsoft, covering fundamentals as well as advanced topics such as AI ethics, big data analytics, autonomous systems, and AI-driven decision-making. Many courses include certificates of completion, which can strengthen professional credentials.

For hands-on experience, platforms like **Kaggle** allow learners to work on real datasets, participate in competitions, and receive feedback from experts. Kaggle also provides tutorials that guide learners from basic concepts to complex machine learning workflows, making it an excellent resource for practical skill development. **Hugging Face Hub** and **Google Colab AI Arena** complement this by providing collaborative environments for training models, experimenting with AI agents, and deploying applications.

Udacity specializes in technology-focused "Nanodegrees," offering programs in machine learning, deep learning, robotics, and applied AI for business. These programs emphasize real-world projects, helping learners gain experience in designing and deploying AI solutions.

For technically inclined users, **GitHub** remains indispensable. It hosts open-source projects, libraries, and repositories for machine learning, natural language processing, and AI development. Modern GitHub integrations, including **GitHub Copilot**, now provide AI-assisted coding, code review, and automated documentation, making learning and development more efficient.

Books continue to be foundational resources. Classic works such as *Deep Learning* by Ian Goodfellow, Yoshua Bengio, and Aaron Courville offer in-depth explanations of neural networks and deep learning concepts. *Artificial Intelligence: A Modern Approach* by Stuart Russell and Peter Norvig remains the authoritative text for understanding AI principles, problem-solving strategies, and applied techniques. For ethical considerations, *Human Compatible* by Stuart Russell and *Ethics of Artificial Intelligence and Robotics* by Patrick Lin, Keith Abney, and Ryan Jenkins provide comprehensive guidance on responsible AI deployment.

Websites and blogs supplement formal learning with practical insights. *Towards Data Science* publishes tutorials and articles on AI, data science, and machine learning applications. *Medium* features professionals sharing real-world experiences, emerging trends, and case studies. Business-oriented insights are available from platforms such as **Harvard Business Review** and **McKinsey & Company**, which explore AI integration across industries and present actionable examples.

Communities and forums are also valuable for feedback and collaborative learning. Platforms like **Stack Overflow** and **Reddit** host active discussions on AI programming, problem-solving, and emerging tools, providing opportunities to interact with professionals and enthusiasts worldwide.

In summary, a wealth of resources exists to support learning and skill development in AI. They cover theory, practical tools, ethical considerations, and real-world applications. Using these resources effectively allows professionals to gain expertise, improve workflows, and confidently integrate AI into their daily work.

www.ingramcontent.com/pod-product-compliance
Lightning Source LLC
Chambersburg PA
CBHW070206230526
45471CB00002B/848